MAI

© 1990 Franklin Watts

First published in the United
States by
Franklin Watts Inc
387 Park Avenue South
New York
N.Y. 10016

Library of Congress Cataloguing-in-Publication Data
Stephen, R. J.
   Tanks, R. J. Stephen.
      p.   cm. — (Picture world)
   Includes index.
   Summary: Discusses the role of tanks and other tracked, armored
vehicles in warfare.
   ISBN 0-531-14012-1
   1. Tanks (Military science)—Juvenile literature.   2. Tank
warfare—Juvenile literature.   3. Armored vehicles, Military—
—Juvenile literature.   [1. Tanks (Military science).   2. Tank
warfare.   3. Armored vehicles, Military.]   I. Title.   II. Series.
UG446.5.B238   1990   89-36501
358′,18—dc20   CIP
                                                                      AC

Printed in Belgium

Series Editor
Norman Barrett

Designed by
K and Co

Photographs by
Finnish Defence Forces
General Dynamics
NATO
Royal Ordnance
Swedish Military Attache
The Tank Museum
U.S. Army
U.S. Department of Defense
Vickers Defence Systems

Technical Consultant
Bernie Fitzsimons

The Picture World of

Tanks

R. J. Stephen

CONTENTS

Franklin Watts

New York • London • Sydney • Toronto

Introduction

Tanks are fighting vehicles used for land warfare. They have tough armor and run on tracks. Main battle tanks have a powerful cannon usually in a rotating turret.

Many other types of armored fighting vehicles are also called tanks. These include tanks for carrying infantry, laying bridges or recovering other vehicles.

▽ A main battle tank rolls along a narrow village street during a military exercise in Europe.

6

▷ A soldier sits astride a Vulcan cannon and surveys the battlefield. The Vulcan is a special gun used by vehicles whose job is to shoot down aircraft.

▽ Battle tanks line up during a maneuver in the desert.

7

Most battle tanks have a crew of three or four — a commander, a driver and a gunner, and usually a loader. Members of the crew have their own compartments, which they reach through hatches in the top of the tank.

△ Each member of a tank crew has his own hatch. Machine-guns are usually mounted on one or more of the hatches. When inside the tank, however, the crew use periscopes and other viewing equipment to observe the outside.

The tank crew operate as a small team. But each tank is usually part of a larger group, which might also include infantrymen and other fighting vehicles.

A tank's commander directs operations according to the overall battle plan. He guides the driver and instructs the gunner.

▽ A tank commander at his machine-gun.

How a tank moves

A tank's engine turns a pair of toothed wheels called driving sprockets. These drive the tracks and force them around the other wheels. The wheels are sprung and have rubber tires to give a smooth ride.

The driver steers the tank by slowing down or stopping the track on the side he wants to turn to.

△ The driving sprocket can be seen at the back, where the tank's engine is located. This tank has seven other wheels on each side. They support the tank on the track.

▷ Because they run on tracks, tanks can move over all kinds of ground.

Firepower

The heavy guns of main battle tanks have the firepower to knock out enemy posts and bombard strong defenses. With special shells, they can also pierce the armor of opposing battle tanks and other heavily armored vehicles.

Smaller tanks can also pack extensive firepower. Some specialized armored vehicles are equipped with rocket or missile launchers.

▽ The turrets of most battle tanks can swivel completely around. This enables the big gun to fire in any direction without the tank having to turn.

△ Finding a target at night is no problem for the modern tank. The gunsight is equipped with a device called a "thermal imager." This forms a picture from the heat given off by the target.

◁ A rocket launcher fitted on the body of a fast-moving tracked vehicle. It can fire rockets to a distance of about 20 miles (30 km).

Main battle tanks

Main battle tanks form the spearhead of an armored division. They are heavy vehicles, weighing 60 tons or more.

Their big guns enable them to strike at the enemy from a distance. Their thick armor protects them as they move about the battlefield.

△ The British-made Chieftain is one of the biggest main battle tanks. It can carry 64 rounds of heavy ammunition for its cannon.

Battle tanks vary in size and design. Some are built for speed, others for sheer power.

On the battlefield, they usually work in small groups, protecting each other as they find cover.

They look for positions where the body of the tank is protected but where the gun can be fired at the enemy.

▽ The Cadillac-Gage Stingray is a light American tank. It weighs only a third as much as a Chieftain, but has the firepower of a main battle tank.

▷ The gunner's controls inside an M-1 Abrams.

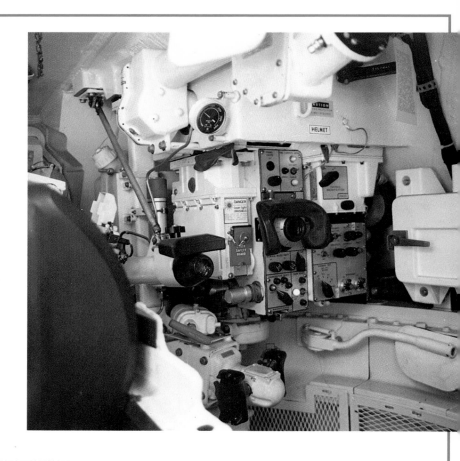

▽ The American-built M-1 is one of the most advanced tanks in service. It has a laser rangefinder, giving it great accuracy, and can move at 45 mph (72 km/h).

△ American M-60
tanks cross a river on a
pontoon bridge. The
driver can be seen
sitting in front, under
the gun, while the
commander, gunner
and loader are in the
turret.

▷ A group of M-60s
on maneuver.
Members of a crew
discuss plans.

△ The Leopard main battle tank, made in West Germany, is used by the armies of several other European countries, as well as Australia and Canada.

▽ The Swedish S-tank is unusual in that it does not have a turret. The gun is aimed by moving the vehicle itself. The tank has the advantage of being low and compact.

△ At 61 tons fully
loaded, the British-
made Challenger is
one of the heaviest
tanks in action today.

▷ Soviet T-72s in
service with the Finnish
Army. The T-72 is used
by Eastern European
armies and in the
Middle East by
countries such as Iraq
and Libya.

Other fighting vehicles

When two opposing armies face each other, tanks and troops clash on the battlefield. Behind the front lines are supply dumps and headquarters.

All kinds of armored vehicles, in addition to main battle tanks, are required to wage war on a battlefield that might cover several hundred square miles.

▽ An M-551 Sheridan reconnaissance tank.

Reconnaissance tanks are light tanks whose chief task is to spot the enemy without being seen themselves. They report back on the enemy's strength and positions.

Other combat vehicles include armored personnel carriers, infantry fighting vehicles, combat engineer vehicles, self-propelled guns and multiple rocket-launchers.

△ An M-113 armored personnel carrier (APC) taking part in a joint American-South Korean exercise. APCs carry defensive machine-guns and are used for transporting infantry on the battlefield.

APCs have been largely replaced in some armies by infantry fighting vehicles. These not only carry fighting troops, but enable them to fight from within their vehicle.

Infantry fighting vehicles (IFVs) can take on main battle tanks as well as other armored vehicles. Sometimes called mechanized infantry combat vehicles (MICVs), they are equipped with automatic cannon and anti-tank missiles.

▽ The M-2 Bradley IFV has a driver in front and a commander and gunner in the turret. Behind them is a troop compartment with room for six or seven infantrymen. All have gun ports that enable them to fire special rifles while protected by the tank's armor.

△ The M-2 is amphibious, being able to propel itself in water by its tracks.

▷ Infantrymen de-bus from the back of an M-2 Bradley.

△ The Chaparral air defense system consists of four Sidewinder heat-seeking missiles mounted on a turntable launcher. This is carried on the rear of a modified M-548 cargo carrier.

◁ The M-548 is used to support heavy self-propelled guns. It carries ammunition and some of the gun crew.

▷ The M-578 recovery vehicle has a pivoting jib crane and a winch. It is used for the battlefield recovery of tanks and other heavy armored vehicles.

▽ A bridgelayer has sections of bridge mounted on a tank chassis. The sections are unfolded across a river or ditch to form a temporary crossing.

Facts

Why they are called tanks

Tanks were first used by the British in 1916, during World War I. While these tough armored vehicles were being designed and built, they were called water tanks to keep their purpose secret.

Working tanks

The Combat Engineer Tractor (CET) is designed to prepare the ground for tanks and other fighting vehicles and perform other battlefield tasks. It is not armed, but has smoke-bomb launchers for its own protection on the battlefield. It has bulldozer equipment attached at the back for earth-moving and clearing obstacles and even laying portable roadways.

△ A CET fires a rocket-propelled anchor. It lodges this in the earth to drag itself out of soft ground.

Speed

Because they run on tracks, tanks are not the fastest of vehicles. But they are not the slow-moving, cumbersome vehicles of earlier days. Modern tanks need speed on the battlefield to avoid getting hit, particularly when making sharp bursts across open land.

The fastest light tank is the Scorpion, with a top speed of 50 mph (81 km/h). The M-1

△ A CET lays a portable "carpet" or roadway with its bulldozer shovel.

△ The Scorpion is the fastest tank.

Abrams is the quickest main battle tank, reaching speeds of 45 mph (72 km/h).

△ The M-1 Abrams is the fastest main battle tank.

All-around vision

Modern tanks are fitted with very advanced technical equipment. The crew must be able to maneuver quickly andd fire their guns while staying safe within the protective armor of their tank. In some tanks, such as the M-1, the commander, has as many as six periscopes, giving him complete all-around vision.

Great tank battles

The tank came into its own during World War II (1939–45). In the early years of the war, the German Panzerkampfwagens, or Panzers, overran much of Europe. But the Panzers met their match in the Soviet T-34s at Kursk in 1943. More than 6,000 armored vehicles took part in the greatest battle in tank history, which resulted in the Germans' withdrawal to save their remaining tanks. Other great tank battles took place between Panzers and British tank divisions in the African desert.

In the Arab-Israeli war of 1973, guided missiles were used in large numbers against tanks for the first time. Almost half of the 6,000 tanks that took part were destroyed in less than three weeks.

△ German Panzer tanks in France during World War II.

Glossary

Amphibious
Able to operate on both land and water.

Armored personnel carrier (APC)
A vehicle used for taking infantry to the battlefield.

Combat engineer tractor (CET)
A vehicle with equipment for special tasks, such as bulldozing or laying roadways.

Driving sprockets
The toothed wheels, turned by the engine, that force the tracks around the other wheels.

Infantry fighting vehicle (IFV)
An advanced form of armored personnel carrier from which troops can fire weapons.

Main battle tank (MBT)
A heavy, well-armored tank used to lead attacking forces.

Mechanized infantry combat vehicle (MICV)
Another name for an infantry fighting vehicle.

Periscope
A device that projects outside the tank's armor and enables crew members to see what is going on.

Pontoon bridge
A temporary bridge set up on the water and supported by flat-bottomed boats or other floats.

Rangefinder
A device used to calculate the distance to a target.

Reconnaissance tank
A light tank used for gathering information on the battlefield.

Recovery vehicle
A tank used for retrieving vehicles that have been put out of action on the battlefield.

Tracks
The continuous belts, made of links, that pass around a tank's wheels.

Turret
The part of the tank that rotates in the body.

Index